Life after Death

28 Days of Refining, Renewing, Restoring and the Refreshing

Copyright © Nicole Dixon Winters

All rights reserved.

Scriptures taken from the Holy Bible, New International Version®, NIV®, The Message®.
Copyright © 1973, 1978, 1984, 2011 by Biblica, Inc.™
The "NIV" and "New International Version" are trademarks registered in the United States Patent and Trademark Office by Biblica, Inc.™

Any names or characters, businesses or places, events or incidents, or resemblance to actual persons, living or dead, or actual events is purely coincidental.

All rights reserved. No part of this publication may be reproduced, stored in a retrieval system, or transmitted in any form or by any means electronic, mechanical, photocopying, recording or otherwise -without the prior permission of the publisher.

ISBN: **0692161198**
ISBN-13: **978-0692161197**

Acknowledgements

This book was written from my heart and based off a true life experience. First and foremost, I want to truly give Honor to my Lord and Savior Jesus Christ who is the head of my life, and the author of my story. He wrote my book before the foundations of the world had even been formed, and everyday that is mentioned in this book was apart of my plan down to every detail. I could have never written this book had it not been for Him feeding me every line, bringing every scripture back to my remembrance, and Him strengthening me through the process. Thank you Lord! I want to thank my mother, my rock in the flesh, my best friend, my strength, and my guide to Christ many years ago, Effie McCollum. Momma thanks for loving me unconditionally, and thank you from the bottom of my heart for everything that you did for my son, how you loved and nurtured him, and how you were there from day one up to the funeral. Thank you for always supporting me no matter what. I love you to the moon and back. To the father of this beautiful baby boy Chanteau Hardin Sr, and the father of my darling daughter Chaneka Hardin. Thank you for being my hero and my strength during the most difficult time of my life. I will always honor you for that! To my sister Tonya Brumfield my protector, and my biggest fan you always come to my rescue my love, and I cherish our relationship. I love you for always being there no matter what. To the man who came and picked up the pieces after his death Eugene L. Winters. The man that gave me 3 beautiful children Stacia Winters, Deja Winters, and Eugene Winters III after my loss and loves my daughter Chaneka Hardin like she is his own. Thank you for your words of encouragement during the process of writing this book. To my sister Mary Hardin who made sure that my son and I had everything that we needed when he passed, and never left my side after the fact. Thank you for making me laugh when I most needed to. To Bishop Robert L. Green for supporting and inspiring me to write in the first place. God bless you Bishop. To Megan Beckett, my sister, my friend, my encourager, my love thank you for staying up with me, listening to me read what I had written and reassuring me that the book was great, but also telling me to never try to "try to get a grip on it" when I would show emotion during this

Life After Death: Growing Past the Pain

process. You reminded me that I was being authentic and real and that my emotions were relevant. I love you baby girl I always have and always will. To Shamika Harris, thank you for all of your support in making my dream a reality. Love you. To Ketrena Jones, my sister thank you for all your help during this process, and always being there. I love you. To Kimberly Fitten, Tameka Reid Sims, Kathy Willis and Adrena Jackson. If it had not been for the Awakening Prayer Retreat, this idea would have not been birthed. Thank you all for believing in me and depositing in me during one of the darkest times in my life! Madonna Awotwi, what a blessing, and a God send. This book is because you believed in me and so I thank you from the bottom of my heart. To Blake Warner one of the best photographers I have seen. Thank you for your time, and professionalism and your support. God Bless you. I wanted to save these people for last, my children Chaneka, Stacia , Deja, and Eugene whom I mentioned above plus my stepchildren Sierra Winters, Nicole Owens, Eugene Winters Jr., Brian Palmer and Brandon Winters, You guys are my everything, my blessings from above. I wouldn't trade any of you for the world. Your my reason I go so hard to be an example before you and to show you that with Christ all things are possible. To the apple of my eye, my granddaughter Amiyah Lanae Nicole Paige, You changed my life, outside of what I feel for God, I have never known a love like this before. You are granny's love bug and will always be. To my granddaughters Ericka, Kierra, and Zuri I love you all so much. Always have and always will. To my unborn grandson granny loves you and can't wait to hold you in my arms. Last but not least thanks to every person that purchased this book, that has experienced the death of a loved one, a marriage, your dreams, your ministry or whatever you loved that you may have lost. This book is for you, to strengthen , and to let you know that your not alone. I love you with the love of Christ and again thank you all.

28 Days of Refining, Renewing, Restoring and the Refreshing

Introduction

"There's a time to be born and a time to die." Birth and death are a part of life, but I want us to go beyond the surface of just the physical aspect of birth, and death and explore other meanings. First, let's deal with the word "birth." Now we all know birth in terms of the emergence of a child from the womb of its mother right. But as we go further birth can also be the "beginning or coming into existence of something." That something can be a relationship, a marriage, the birth of a ministry, the beginning of a pregnancy and so on and so forth. When we dig a little deeper into the word "death," it can mean the action or fact of dying or being killed; the end of the life of a person; but it can also mean "the destruction or permanent end of something." That something can be a marriage that resulted in a divorce, a relationship that ended, a pregnancy that resulted in a miscarriage, and even a ministry that is stunted.

The start or birth of these events in our life can be some of the most memorable, happiest and fulfilling times in our lives, but the death of the same events can be the most painful, unimaginable, difficult, and horrific times of our lives. When these trying times come they are usually accompanied by a few companions which are fear, frustration, confusion, sadness, hopelessness, guilt, shame, and let's not leave out grief. These are the times in life that we experience loss and the grief that follows seems too much to bear. There is no blueprint for how we are to grieve or for how long one grieves, but it is vitally important that we do. Grief is a process that we must go through to be healed and find peace with the situation. Sometimes we can grieve and sometimes we're not able to due to all the emotions that accompany grief. Grief comes with a multiplicity of emotions and it becomes difficult to bear it all at once and just that

Life After Death: Growing Past the Pain

thought of the event causes pain to set in. Have you ever injured yourself and at first there is no pain, and as soon as you start to ponder on what just happened, suddenly, the pain kicks in? This is what happens when we experience a tragic event in our lives maybe it's the loss of a loved one or a career and finances, maybe it's the divorce or the report from the doctor. No matter the circumstance, when we begin to ponder on the events, our emotions kick in and they are always accompanied by pain.

The emotions that arise when we have lost a loved one are common especially when it is someone close, someone or something we love. Maybe it's a divorce after many years and coming to the realization that your life is about to change can feel scary. Loneliness and the thought of starting over again scares you and learning how to live without someone you love starts to feel overwhelming. This is when going on with our lives seems impossible to even imagine. It can be someone close to us that have committed suicide, or a miscarriage after anticipating the arrival of your child. A dream you had that has died out due to fear of failing, or the close of a ministry that you put your all into. The destruction or permanent end to anything that we have invested time, care and love into can cause us to feel the same effects that we experience in the grieving process. Sometimes we come out of this process of grief and at times we get stuck there and don't know how to move forward and go on with our lives.

As you go through the next 28 days, know that this is not some magical book that promises you will be healed and on your way. This is a book based on my own personal experience with loss, and how I turned to God to get through. This experience will be different for every reader but know that there is something in here for everyone, and if we apply the principles stated, we will have the tools needed to not only deal with the pain but grow past it.

28 Days of Refining, Renewing, Restoring and the Refreshing

My Story

Never in a million years did I ever think that I would have to bury the son I so desperately prayed for at 1 years old. He was playing when he took his last breath in my arms.

Life After Death: Growing Past the Pain

He was always laughing and when he smiled he did this thing where he would stick his tongue out of his mouth, and with his last breath there he sat, on my left knee with his tongue hanging out of his mouth minus the smile that use to greet me. My neighbor rushed in performing CPR on his lifeless body, and all I could do or knew to do was cry out to God "please don't take him from me please!" Maybe it was the way that I asked, or the fact that I was crying so hard that God couldn't make out my words, because by the time that we arrived at the hospital he was gone.

My first born, the love of my life, Chanteau Maurice Hardin Jr. For the next few months depression, confusion and frustration would become my default settings, and I had gotten use to having them around. My family and friends tried as hard as they could to cheer me up, but I had decided that there was no reason for me to cheer up. I believed in God and that he had blessed me with my son, but somehow, I couldn't wrap my mind around being blessed one minute by God, and the next minute the same God that made me smile, made me cry. Everyone kept telling me that God was with me and that He loved and cared for me, but at this point to me it really didn't matter. All I knew is that my baby was gone and so was every ounce of joy, happiness and life for that matter.

28 Days of Refining, Renewing, Restoring and the Refreshing

"He was my little baby boy
He was mommas little pride and joy
But you went away and took part of me and left my heart so cold
Why did you have to take my son?
He was my first and only one
Now I'm left with only memories
I want to know
Why me
Why did I go through this pain?
Why me
I'll never forget the day that I had to lay me precious son to rest
The pain was all through my chest
To see him lay there so lifeless
Father answer me there's one thing I want to know
Why me

To get through this I had to stop
Include my God and walk the walk
Cause I found myself just given up I wouldn't eat or talk
But then he came and took my hand
To try and make understand
That death has no true season
And my son was here for a reason
Why me
Why did I go through this pain?
Why me
I'll never forget the day
That I had to lay my precious son to rest
The pain was all through my chest
To see him lay there so lifeless
Father answer me there's one thing I want to know
Why me"

Life After Death: Growing Past the Pain

This was my heart on paper. My pain wrapped in a melody, and I had no idea that creativity could be birthed out of pain.

While in the emergency room at the hospital, the Chaplin came in to provide comfort but there was nothing that anyone could do or say that would make a difference at this point. The doctor came in and explained that he had bled to death due to a previous procedure that was performed 7 days prior. On the night of February 26th, 1993, my boyfriend was in the kitchen cooking, I was sitting on the couch in the Livingroom and my son next to me on the floor playing with his toys. He got up from the floor and came and sat straddled on my lap and laid his head on my chest. I was under the impression that he just wanted to cuddle since that's what we did often, but then suddenly, he began to throw up blood clots and I panicked screaming for his dad to come and assist. He came out of the kitchen and grabbed him out of my arms, and all I saw was my son laying across both his father's arms limp. He didn't appear to be breathing and so I called 911, and my sister that lived around the corner. My sister beat the paramedics to my house and by the time they made it he was up and breathing. They put him in the ambulance and off to the hospital we went. While sitting in the ambulance, I had a vision of me sitting at a funeral but never dreamed that it would be my son's.

The doctors found that he had swallowed what looked like a nickel but was much thinner. They took a foreign object, and through his mouth, they extracted the object not realizing that they tore his esophagus which caused internal bleeding. The doctor gave him iron and kept him overnight. I was told not to worry about the discoloration of his bowels because the iron would cause this, but it was actually caused by the internal bleeding.

God is so strategic

Once he was released the next day, I felt a strong urge to go to Chicago where my mom was. God didn't allow me to go through this on my own. I had been residing in Waukesha, WI when all of this took place and wanted to go be with my mom once he was released from the hospital. On March 1st, my Greyhound bus Departing from Wisconsin was scheduled to leave at 2:00 pm going to Chicago. I lived 30 minutes away from the bus station, and by the time I looked up, it was already 2:00 pm and I was still at home. I started to cancel the trip because I thought I would never make it to the bus on time, but the urge was so strong I would try to make it anyway. Just when I made it to the bus station at 2:40, the bus driver was about to pull off. The departure had been delayed just for me. Side note: isn't it amazing how God takes time to make things work out for us! He knew I couldn't go through this alone.

We made it to Chicago and the plan was to stay at my mom's for a week and then return home to Wisconsin, but God had another plan that would turn my world upside down. For the next 5 days, we were at my mom's and everything seemed to be going well. My mother was so happy to see us, especially Baby Sean which is the nickname that we gave my son. My mother had a special relationship with him. They had such a connection from the first day I brought him home to her house from the hospital.

It was Friday, March 6th and I had plans to take Baby Sean to my best friend's daughter's birthday party. I was at my mom's along with 5 of my cousins and my auntie Barbara, who had come to visit with us. My mom had just left to go see some friends, and I told myself that I would sit down for a few minutes and then get him dressed for the party. As I sat on the couch, he did his usual by sitting next to me on the floor playing with his toys. He began to cry out and I asked him what was wrong. He climbed up on my knee, dropped his head back and my cousin said he's blue in the face.

Life After Death: Growing Past the Pain

He leaned forward with his tongue hanging out of his mouth, and that was the moment I lost my baby boy.

We made it to the emergency room, and with my family, friends, and the father of my son present, somehow, I still felt alone. Everyone was going back into the room to see his lifeless body, but I could not and told myself I would not go back to see him. After about an hour I finally decided to go back. His dad was laying across his tiny body barely able to breath. He was crying so hard that you could no longer make out his words or maybe I was just in a daze. When I walked in, there was one drop of blood on his nose and at first, I started to break down, but as I got closer to his bed he looked like he was asleep, and for some strange reason I felt a sense of peace.

Here I am, 20 years old having to plan the funeral of my son at only 13 months old. This was the hardest thing I ever had to go through to this very day, and I had no idea how I would make it through this. Chanteau Maurice Hardin Sr., his father was my hero. He told me that I didn't have to worry about a thing that he would take care of it all. How selfless, because he's hurting as well, but it was more important to him for him to stay strong for me. I will always honor him for that.

After the funeral I didn't know what to think, say or do so I went to the church of the pastor that officiated his service. The name of the church was "God Never Fails Ministry." They were having a revival which revival is defined as "an improvement in the condition or strength of something." God knew what he was doing. I joined the church that day, and that was the start of not only a beautiful relationship but my journey to healing.

As you journey through this devotional with me, you might be dealing with a recent loss, or still trying to cope with a not so recent loss. Either way that it goes, we will embark on this journey of Refining, Renewing, Restoring and Refreshing together.

The Refining

When I was a high school student, I felt the worse part of school were the test we had to take. What was even worse than the test were the pop quizzes that the teacher would give because they were unexpected. Majority of the time I was never prepared for the pop quiz, but I had no choice in the matter, it had to be done. My palms would be sweaty, I began to doubt what I had already known and being honest, I was overcome by fear. I always had the appearance of being smart and confident to my peers, but these moments of testing revealed my weaknesses.

As Christians, we experience the same when our faith is being tested. We already know God and that he is able, and to our family and friends we appear confident in our faith, but as soon as the unexpected test comes in the form of a diagnosis, or the notice in the mail, an unexpected death of a loved one, divorce or the loss of a career we begin to doubt what we know God to be. Once the pain begins to set in, our weaknesses are revealed as fear, lack of faith, hopelessness, anger, frustration, guilt, and doubt.

1 Peter tell us that "fiery trials come to refine our faith," and if we know anything about the process of refining gold it has to be put through the fire.

Gold goes through a process called smelting where it is put through extreme heat and during this process the impurities rise to the surface. The last step is called refining where the heat in this process burns away the impurities, and the gold is purified. It is the same with us. God loves us too much to leave us where we are so when we find ourselves going through the fire (trials) divorce, the loss of a loved one, a bad report from the doctor etc., and our impurities rise to the surface.

Life After Death: Growing Past the Pain

Fear, guilt, shame, hopelessness, anger, frustration, doubt, and all other emotions that we experience during difficult times., but this is sometimes hard to swallow because this process doesn't feel good; but the gold is only in the fire a small amount of time, and when this process is finished, the gold is now pure.

When I was going through that refining process, it was very difficult for me. I didn't realize that this is what was taking place, all I knew is the hurt and pain that I was experiencing and I remember thinking I would not make it through this. It felt like this was too much for one person to have to endure. Without my family, friends and most importantly my Lord I would have never made it through. It was all a part of my process, and eventually, I came out just as the gold, shining and pure. It is my prayer that you have the same experience and that you can come to the realization that this is only part of your process, and you too will make it through.

28 Days of Refining, Renewing, Restoring and the Refreshing

Day 1

Proverbs 3:5-6 New King James Version (NKJV)
5 Trust in the Lord with all your heart, and lean not on your own understanding;

6 In all your ways acknowledge Him, And He shall direct your paths.

About 6 years ago, I and my friend hopped in a car and drove to New York. While enjoying conversations and the view of land we had never seen before, we unexpectedly came upon a tunnel. I had never driven through a tunnel before, and I really didn't know what to expect. Upon entering the tunnel, I was surrounded by darkness and I knew that we would eventually reach the end of the tunnel, but I entertained thoughts of no end. As fear begins to consume me, all conversation ceased. This was the longest 3 minutes of my life. We couldn't see what was ahead, only what was directly in front of us. I recall thinking "what if we never make it out of here." As we continued, all I could focus on was the darkness that was staring at me. After about 2 minutes we began to see what appeared to be a little speck of light ahead. From where I sat, it was the size of a rice grain but just that little bit of light gave me some hope, but it didn't say how much longer I had until I was out. As we drove, the light began to enlarge and the closer we got to the end of the tunnel the bigger the speck of light grew. Once we reached the end of the tunnel, it was like we suddenly busted out of this dark place, into the presence of this bright sky and the light was shining all around us. The light had been awaiting our arrival and was there all along; we had the task of just making it through to the end. Enduring the darkness, but all the while focusing on what was ahead instead of what was right in front of us. It was beautiful, and all though traveling through this tunnel of darkness seemed like an eternity, it had a beautiful ending.

When my son died, I entered this dark place that I never thought I would escape. It felt as if that was the end of not only his existence

Life After Death: Growing Past the Pain

but my very own. At first, all I could see was the image of him lying there lifeless, and thoughts of that day played in my head constantly. Every word spoken that day became a song I put on repeat in my mind. I rehearsed the lyrics to this song, and as the days went by I told myself that I would never move past this, and I would never have another child. I had never experienced hurt to this magnitude in my life, and I never wanted to feel like this again. I couldn't see past the pain that was staring at me to even begin to realize that there was light ahead.

It wasn't until I gave it over to the Lord that I began to come out of this dark place. I know this might sound cliché, but it was when I went to church the day of his funeral that I began to see that little speck of light. I didn't know how much longer I had to suffer with the pain that came from losing him, but I had hope just as I did when I first saw the speck of light while driving through the tunnel.

As you are traveling through this refining process, it will be dark, scary, and you might be telling yourself just as I did that there is no end. I want you to know that you are not alone, and this is the time to do just as the scripture says which is "trust in the Lord with all your heart" meaning to confide in Him and to be secure in His promises. We must trust in the fact that He is the best knower for our lives and that He is able to do for us just what he said he will do. That we are not alone and that according to every promise He has made to be there with us and for us, that He will do just that and at the same time do what is best for us. Leaning to our own understanding is like trying to perform surgery on ourselves. We must seek him for direction and advice in not only the difficult times but anytime we are unsure of what to do or which way to go. He loves us and will never steer us wrong.

We must also acknowledge Him as Lord over our lives, and the creator of our lives "in all our ways." We must begin, continue, and end every situation, endeavor, decision, plan, and circumstance with God. He planned out our lives a long time ago and knows when things will begin and the ending of them. Relying on ourselves has always been the ruin of man since the beginning of time. He must be included in all our affairs because He is the author of such.

28 Days of Refining, Renewing, Restoring and the Refreshing

Prayer

Lord, we come to You today with full hope and trust in you. Knowing you are the only help through these difficult times and that you are also the giver of our peace through any storm. Lord, we lean on not our own understanding, but we lean on the very fact that you will direct our paths. Today we will cast our cares on you for your word says we ought to do so because you care for us. We ask that you send the comfort of your Holy Spirit and lead and direct us in every aspect of our lives. We love you Lord and we could never make it without you. We give you all the honor because it is due. We give You all the glory because it belongs to You, and we give You all the praise because You deserve it. In Jesus Mighty and Majestic name, Amen.

Life After Death: Growing Past the Pain

Day 2

Psalm 145:18-19 New King James Version (NKJV)

18 The Lord is near to all who call upon Him, to all who call upon Him in truth.
19 He will fulfill the desire of those who fear Him; He also will hear their cry and save them.

After Jesus had been crucified and buried in the tomb, Mary Magdalene went to the tomb while it was still dark and saw that the stone had been taken away from the tomb. She ran to go tell Peter and the other disciples that Jesus' body was no longer there, and she didn't know where they had taken Him. Can you imagine the pain she must have felt while still grieving the death of her Lord, and now not being able to locate his body?

So, she made it back to the tomb and Peter and the other disciples saw for themselves that the body was no longer there, and they turned and left. Mary stayed weeping outside of the tomb. Mary looked inside the tomb and saw two angels sitting there where the body had been laid and they asked her "Woman why are you weeping?" She responded saying that "they had taken her Lord and she doesn't know where they have laid him."

Next, Mary see's someone standing there and thinks it is the gardener when it is Jesus. Now, we know that Mary Magdalene knew Jesus and even had a relationship with him. She loved Jesus and was present at the crucifixion but at this moment and in her grief she didn't recognize Him. This is the same with us when we are in pain. We get so blinded by the pain that we don't realize that Jesus is right there with us. We know Him and love Him but don't see or recognize His presence.

So, Mary thinks it is the gardener and ask "Sir, if you have carried Him away, please tell me where you have laid Him, and I will take Him away." Jesus then says to her "Mary!" She responds and says "Rabboni"

28 Days of Refining, Renewing, Restoring and the Refreshing

Which is to say, teacher. Of all the names that she could have called Him especially after seeing Him crucified, dead and buried, she calls him teacher after seeing that He has risen. Let me suggest to your thinking that Mary called Him who she needed Him to be because she needed instructions and the role of a teacher is to instruct right. Mary was in pain, blinded by her pain and not knowing what to do next.

I didn't know what to do, which way to go, and even in my moments of doubt I still knew to call on the name of Jesus. When my son stopped breathing, I cried out to God. When I felt like I was about to lose my mind, I cried out to God. I was in need of a healer and a savior and that's what I called Him. I didn't realize that He had answered, but when I look back I know he was present because I remained in my right mind, I didn't fall into a deep depression, and it's because God kept me. I was in need of direction and He sent the pastor that funeralized my son to help me during my time of pain.

When we are going through and don't know what to do, we must call Him by who we need Him to be believing that He is near and willing. If it is financial difficulty, then we call Him provider. If we are sick, we call Him Healer. The scripture says to "call on Him in truth, and He will hear our cry and save us."

God is with us during these difficult times. All we must do is call upon the name of the Lord. No matter how alone you may feel He promised to never leave us. Today, rest in the fact that God is near to the brokenhearted, and rest in the fact that He will save you. I admonish you to call Him who you need Him to be in your life on today.

I didn't know what to do, which way to go, and even in my moments of doubt I still knew to call on the name of Jesus.

Life After Death: Growing Past the Pain

When my son stopped breathing, I cried out to God. When I felt like I was about to lose my mind, I cried out to God. I need a healer and a savior and that what I called Him.

Prayer

Father, today we call upon your name in our time of grief, and we trust that during this process you will be right here with us. Lord help us to feel your hand on our situation and know that we need your comfort and your healing Father. Today we call you who we need, you to be and that is a teacher. Lord show us what to do next, order our footsteps in you. Lord, we trust you and believe in your Word. We thank and praise you in advance for healing and peace and we pray all these things in your son Jesus Might and Majestic Name Amen.

Day 3

Ecclesiastes 3:1-2 NLT
1. *For everything, there is a season, a time for every activity under heaven.*

It is evident that we live in a world that is constantly changing. Just look back over the last 5 years of your life and see just how much has changed in prices, politics, our bodies, the environment, and even our families. Change is a constant, and sometimes scary and uncomfortable. Change can hurt if we let it. Change can cause us to be confused and question what we thought we once knew. There's a quote I once heard "as soon as I think I have the answer, the question changes." When Baby Sean died I thought that I had much more time than I did. I just knew that I would get the opportunity to watch him grow into a teen and then a man. The one thing that I realized is that just as my life was planned out so was His and there was an allotted amount of time that I was given to nurture him, love and care for him, and when that season was up, so was my time with him. We must make the most of each season because just as we are sure that one day winter will end, and spring begins; we know that seasons in our lives are going to change and how that change looks for us is unknown.

Losing him changed my life forever, but I take solace in the fact that I spent my time with him well. In this refining stage, it is okay to have your emotions, it's natural to feel in this process. The thing is that we don't get stuck here and that we reflect on the time that we have had with our loved ones. If this process your experiencing is due to an ailment or an illness, don't lose sight of who God is or has been in your life because in our pain we will mistake the pain for punishment and the fact of the matter is, it is a part of our process. Remember and rest in the fact that God loves us and is allowing these hardships and trials as a means to refine our faith.

Life After Death: Growing Past the Pain

Know that at some point everything in life changes just as the seasons, but there is one constant that we have to lean on in those moments of change and that is God. The scripture says that He is the same yesterday, today and forever (Hebrews 13:8). So in your grief hold on to His unchanging hands, and know that if He brought you through difficulties before, He can do it again. Trust in Him and you will make it through this.

Prayer

Father, we come to you today asking for strength to make it through this process, and that while we are going through that you be with us to comfort and keep us. Help us to rest in the fact that you are with us and that when we come through this process we will be as pure gold, trusting and believing that you were with us through it all and you never left us. We love you Father and we can't make it without out you. We trust you and we stand on your word. Heal us Oh Lord and we will be healed. Save us and we will be saved for you are our praise. No matter what the issues we know that there is not one problem on earth that Heaven can't solve, and we pray these things in Jesus Mighty and Majestic name Amen.

Day 4
John 9:1-3 New King James Version

9 Now as Jesus passed by, He saw a man who was blind from birth. 2 And His disciples asked Him, saying, "Rabbi, who sinned, this man or his parents, that he was born blind?"
3 Jesus answered, "Neither this man nor his parents sinned, but that the works of God should be revealed in him.

One of the emotions that we experience during our process is guilt or we begin to place blame just as they did in this scripture. While I was going through this process, guilt set in and I blamed myself by saying if only I had fought for the hospital to keep him longer, or if I had stayed at home he would still be here. Maybe God took him because of a sin I committed because I was not married when I gave birth to him. This man was born blind and the first question asked was if he or his parents had sinned and caused him to be born blind. We tend to think that those that sin greatly also suffer greatly, but there are some who suffered much and have sinned little.

Even though it becomes difficult to accept, we must consider the fact that God has a plan that included us all, and we must hold on to the fact that whatever the situation is that we are facing whether it is a marriage failing, loss, sickness, a miscarriage, or someone we love committed suicide, Christ is with us and His works shall be revealed in our situation. There are others around us that don't know Him but will come to know Him as a healer once they see us fully recovered or see those of us that have lost a loved one at peace with the situation; then they will come to know Him as the giver of peace. God loves us, and it is important to hold on to that while going through. Don't lose sight of who He is or has been to you and don't allow yourself to get caught up by guilt because it is not the way of the Lord.

Life After Death: Growing Past the Pain

The book of Ecclesiastes chapter 3 tells us that there is a time to be born and a time to die. This is a harsh reality because no one wants to lose someone they love, but death is inevitable and it's an appointment that no one can reschedule. If we began to look at it this way, this will stop us from blaming ourselves and feeling guilty. Death is a part of life, so we must not allow it to stop us from living once we have had the experience with it.

Prayer

Lord, I come before you today asking that You regulate my thoughts and that You remove all guilt or shame that I may be feeling. Father God, I trust in your timing and in your plan for my life and I pray that you help me to cope with and move beyond this pain that I am experiencing. Help me to accept the process and not view it as punishment. Cover and keep me Lord in Jesus name I pray Amen.

Day 5

1 Peter 1:6-7 NLT

So be truly glad. There is wonderful joy ahead, even though you must endure many trials for a little while. 7 These trials will show that your faith is genuine. It is being tested as fire tests and purifies gold—though your faith is far more precious than mere gold. So when your faith remains strong through many trials, it will bring you much praise and glory and honor on the day when Jesus Christ is revealed to the whole world.

In this process, it is easy to lose sight of God and anything that will bring us joy. We think that God is punishing us and we sometimes find ourselves upset with Him. Know that God is not punishing you, and He truly loves you. This is the time to draw near to God; We have to let him in knowing that He is the author and finisher of our faith. Our faith starts remains and ends with Him

It is so important that we remain strong in our faith during these times. It sounds difficult to focus on the joy ahead as the scripture states especially when you have pain in front of you, but trust me when I tell you that there was much joy ahead of me, and many blessings awaiting. I just had to hold on to my faith and remember who God had been to me before, during moments that I had experienced pain in the past. There were times that I felt alone, but I know now that there was no way in the world I made it out of those hard times by myself. God was with me through it all and if you trust in Him, He will be there with you as well. So hold on your joy is coming. No matter what it feels like or looks like, not only are you coming out as pure gold, but your faith will be shown as genuine to your Father in heaven.

Life After Death: Growing Past the Pain

Earlier we talked about the reefing of gold and the impurities that surface when we are being tested as gold. I had all type of impurities rise to the surface that I didn't even know existed in me when my son passed away. I always considered myself to be strong and fearless. I lived in and walked the streets of Chicago and I had to be tough, so I didn't fear anything, or at least I didn't think so. I started to experience fear, guilt, anger, and frustration which are all impure thoughts, which in turn weakened my faith. So I had to go through the refining process because the truth of the matter is I stopped believing in myself and started to doubt God. I regarded myself as being incapable of being a mother because this had to be my fault. But then God started to show up, sending me comforting words through others, giving me peace when I thought I was about to lose my mind, and once these impure thoughts left me, I could actually feel His presence. In this process, these impurities were burnt up, and eventually, just as the gold my thoughts were pure, and I was free to believe again. This fiery trial that I was enduring was truly refining my faith.

Today, reflect back to a time that you were happy before any of this began and ask God to help you to get back there. Be willing to release these impure thoughts that come and weaken your faith and steal your joy. Lean on God today and trust that He is with you through the process. Picture yourself loving, and believing again and most importantly, picture yourself growing past the pain.

28 Days of Refining, Renewing, Restoring and the Refreshing

Prayer

Father, I thank you for the trials that have come to refine my faith. I thank you that you never gave up on me even when I began to doubt you. Thank you for loving me, and being with me through all of my pain. It is my prayer that you will continue to increase my faith, and help me in my unbelief. I love you Lord and I trust you and I ask all these things in Jesus name Amen.

Father have your way in my life on today. Restore me and renew me while I go through these trials. I know that you are with me and that you will never leave me. Create in me a clean heart, and renew the right Spirit in me. Restore my joy and help me to be at peace with the situation. I ask these things in Jesus name Amen.

Life After Death: Growing Past the Pain

Day 6

John 16:32

"Yet I am not alone, for my Father is with me."

Within the first couple of months, I would feel this sense of loneliness, even in a room filled with people. I began to isolate myself feeling as if it was best for me to be alone. The fact of the matter is that this was the wrong time to be alone because I had all the time in the world to ponder on the negative and start to fall into a depression which can be damaging to the mental wellbeing of anyone causing you to feel unwanted, and empty. But thanks be to God that He was with me in Spirit and sent people to be with me in the flesh that would exemplify His love and care for me during this difficult time.

My Family and my friend were there with me and for me day in and day out. My cousin Haji, Kelvin, and my friend Mary whom I consider my sister never left my side. They made me laugh and remember the good times in which laughter can be your umbrella in any storm. Just being in their presence was therapeutic for me because they were always positive, and they kept me busy. It is good to have people around you that encourage you and keep you uplifted, and never forget that even though you can't see Him God is ever present.

If your experiencing feelings of loneliness, I would admonish you to be in the presence of those whom you love. We have a tendency to push our loved ones away during difficult times, but I challenge you to do the opposite. Maybe it's your husband or a family member, a friend or someone that you can go to for support. Laugh, smile, remember and even cry if you have to, just be sure that you don't do it alone. This period of refining can be difficult, and uncomfortable, but know that you don't have to go through it alone.

28 Days of Refining, Renewing, Restoring and the Refreshing

Embrace the presence of the Lord, and the presence of those whom He sent to provide comfort during your time of bereavement.

Today, thank God for being with you and if you're feeling alone then pray that He allows you to feel His presence, and pray that He sends someone in the physical so you don't feel alone. Understand that the people He will send may probably already be around you; just make sure that you leave yourself open for them to come in. Spend some quality time with a friend or a loved one, it just might make you feel better. If today is not a good day for you then try tomorrow. As long as you don't give up.

Prayer

Father, I'm coming to you because I feel alone. Please help me to not go into a place of isolation and push away those whom you send in my life to be with me and be a support to me. Father bring the warmth of relationships into my life and cover my thoughts with hope. Please send your love into my heart. I know you are alive in all I experience, and I thank you for always being by my side. I give thanks for all those who love me, and all those you sent that care. Help me to open up and receive your hope in my heart, to embrace your loving kindness for me. I rest in knowing your love and compassion flows in my life, and that I dwell safely in you. I thank you, Father, that I am not alone. In Jesus name, I pray Amen.

Life After Death: Growing Past the Pain

Day 7

Matthew 5:4 Blessed are those who mourn, for they will be comforted

I remember when I was just a little girl and I would fall and scrape my knee or elbow my mom would say "let me kiss it and make it all better." After she kissed the wound, she would say "it's all better now," as she's wrapped her warm arms around my petite frame. I would get up and wipe my tears after being comforted by her, and go back to playing as if nothing ever happened. I thought my mother had some type of magical kiss because in my mind the pain had subsided. In reality, the pain was still present, and it was her comfort and compassion that made me feel as if I could go on.

It is the same with God but we have to be in a place where are open to accepting His comfort. When we get all scraped up and bruised by life and are in pain (mourning) our Father says let me make it all better, and as He wraps His warm arms around us, the pain begins to subside, and we too are able to go on with our lives. The comfort that we feel comes by way of the Holy Spirit. We must believe that God sees our tears and knows our pain and that He will show compassion for His children. When I began to cry out to God and had made up in my mind that He was the only one that could ease my pain, I felt that magic kiss all over again, and soon after I was able to go on with my life, live again, work and have other children. This refining process is very difficult, but just as the gold you come out shining brightly.

Today, trust Him and invite Him in while you are grieving; allow him to comfort you knowing that He cares for you.

28 Days of Refining, Renewing, Restoring and the Refreshing

Prayer

Father, I come before you today first and foremost wanting to say thank you. I thank you for being with me through my process and sending the comfort of your Holy Spirit. Holy Spirit I welcome you in my life and I am open to receive from you the comfort my father promised in my time of mourning. Lord, I love you and I can't live without you, and I pray all these things in your Son Jesus name. Amen

The Renewing

We are now entering the second stage of this process which is called the "renewing." Renewing defined is to make new again; repairing; re-establishing; repeating; renovating. The renewing stage almost has to take place in the stage of refining, because unless the mind is renewed, we will see the pain as a punishment and not part of our process. This will cause us to become stuck, hindered, and living in fear and guilt. Always worrying about what could go wrong, never considering what could go right.

When a married couple renews their vows sometimes it's after a rough patch and they want to reaffirm their commitment to one another. We have to do the same thing when it comes to ourselves after a rough patch that we have been through. We have to reaffirm or recommit to our dreams, our visions, and our goals and most importantly we have to keep living. Realizing that death is a part of life was the key to me being able to live after my loss. Changing my attitude and thoughts toward my pain, allowed me to finally move beyond it and find a sense of joy, and in the process, my mind was renewed.

28 Days of Refining, Renewing, Restoring and the Refreshing

Life After Death: Growing Past the Pain

Day 8

Ephesians 4:23 Instead, let the Spirit renew your thoughts and attitudes.

For a split second, I began to question God, the epitome of love that I had always known Him to be. I asked myself "how can God love me, and take someone I love from me? What did I do to make God punish me like this?" I was a little upset with God, and in my mind, I had done something to cause his death. My mind became an enemy that kept taunting me, reminding me of my pain. My mind was the judge, jury, and executioner and I was on trial. My mind found me guilty of the murder of my son and I was sentenced to life in prison without the possibility of parole. I started to believe that I was guilty, but I didn't want to spend the rest of my life in prison so I appealed the court's decision. I took the matter before the Supreme court, the highest court and He found some discrepancies in the case against me. The judge granted me a new trial and the conviction was overturned and I was set free.

I was vindicated and the Lord was the reason. I was not the cause of my son's death. I had to change my way of thinking concerning his death and the entire situation. I needed a renewing of the mind and God gave me just that. Instead of looking at myself as being the cause of his death, I started to tell myself that I was the reason for his life (along with God). Instead of me looking at the short amount of time I got to spend with my son, I looked at the quality of time I spent with him. I no longer viewed his death and the pain from his death as a punishment. I began to see it as part of my process, my journey and realized that this journey called life is not always a smooth one. There will be some moments that are breathtaking, and some that will take your breath away. Either way, it goes I have the memory of my baby, and I got to love him for 13 whole months.

28 Days of Refining, Renewing, Restoring and the Refreshing

This type of thinking comes from renewing your mind, but understand that you can't accomplish this on your own, and as the scripture stated "let the Spirit renew your thoughts and attitudes" and the word "let" meaning we have to allow the Spirit to work in our mind and by doing so, we change the way we not only view trials that arise, but we also change our attitude toward a situation and how we choose to handle it.

Today, take those negative thoughts and look for the positives and allow yourself to be led by the Spirit in your thinking.

Prayer

Father, I come before you today surrendering my thoughts unto you. Holy Spirit regulates and guides my thoughts, renew my mind and help me through this process of renewing. Lord give me strength for the journey and the wisdom to know the difference between pain and punishment Lord I trust your plan for my life, and I know your plans were not of evil but for my good. Help me to always hone in on what you're doing in my life and not why you're doing what you doing. Lord I love with all that is within me and I thank you for all that you've blessed me with. In Jesus name, I pray, Amen.

Life After Death: Growing Past the Pain

Day 9

Mark 11:22-25 New Living Translation (NLT)

22 Then Jesus said to the disciples, "Have faith in God. 23 I tell you the truth, you can say to this mountain, 'May you be lifted up and thrown into the sea,' and it will happen. But you must really believe it will happen and have no doubt in your heart. 24 I tell you, you can pray for anything, and if you believe that you've received it, it will be yours. 25 But when you are praying, first forgive anyone you are holding a grudge against, so that your Father in heaven will forgive your sins, too.

I use to tell people all the time that when you forgive others that may have wronged you, you forgive them for yourself and not for them. Oh, how wrong was I. This is a selfish mentality and I had to get over it quickly because it was not of God. When we forgive others, it is for the other person as well as ourselves. Everyone doesn't know how to apologize, and some are sorry and will never admit it. Either way, it goes they are struggling with the issue themselves, and when we forgive them, we remove their guilt and shame and free them as well. That is exactly what Christ did for us. We were guilty of sin, but Him going to the cross took all of the guilt and shame away. He freed us because of His love for us, and so we must remember that love we have for those that may not treat us right, and forgive them because we have been forgiven much.

I prayed and asked God to heal me from my pain, my thoughts, and the unspoken feelings that I had toward certain people. I knew that it was going to take faith in God to get this mountain of guilt, and anger from in front of me, but being honest with you, I prayed these

28 Days of Refining, Renewing, Restoring and the Refreshing

prayers of mine doubting in my heart that I would get past this. I had some days where I was up and some days that I was down. I was wavering in my faith and growing weak. As previously stated, I was free in my mind and knew I wasn't guilty of the death of my son, but somehow these feelings would come to visit every now and then.

The scripture states that "we can pray for anything, and believe it and it will be ours," but I was lost because I would pray and still some days nothing would happen. Then I realized that I was harboring ill feelings toward a few people. I was upset with my father because he lived in the same city as me and yet the first time he ever saw my son was at his funeral. So I had made up in my mind that I would never forgive him and I didn't want to talk to him ever again. Then I was upset with my auntie because as close as we were, she overslept the day of the funeral and never made it. I never took into consideration what my aunt and my dad were going through, all I could focus on was my pain.

It takes a lot of energy to hold a grudge, and I was mentally exhausted. I called my auntie and told her how I felt, and she explained to me why she didn't make it, and I understood because she was dealing with some pain of her own. It wasn't that she didn't want to be there with me because she did and I knew she loved me, but what she was dealing with was bigger than anything that I could have imagined. We talked, we cried and we laughed, and I forgave her. It was just that simple, one conversation and all of that anger were gone and our relationship had been restored, and it felt so good. As far as my father is concerned, I never got an apology and that's okay because we have to be able to see things for what they are. He had never been there for me any other time in my life and I didn't have a close-knit relationship with him. I talked to him and told him how I felt, and he really didn't have a response.

Life After Death: Growing Past the Pain

So I had to move forward and accept the fact that not everyone will apologize and that's okay. Forgive them anyway and accept the apology that I will never get.

I'm glad I made it right and God was answering my prayer and renewing my mind and restoring relationships just in the nick of time. Just a couple of years after I made up with my aunt, she passed away. I did not have to carry the guilt of not making things right with her. My father ended up taking ill and I, along with my mother was the ones to care for him during that time.

Today you might be upset with your spouse over the divorce, or there may be someone you blame for the situation. Whatever the case makes it right today, and forgive them, and then your Father in heaven will hear your prayers and if you believe that you've received it, it is yours. Carrying un-forgiveness on top of your pain will not only wear you down, but it may stop your forward mobility altogether. Let it go it's not worth your future.

Prayer

Lord I come before you today with my hands stretched out, for you are the only help that I know. Lord help me to forgive myself, and anyone that has offended me. Help me to love as you love and forgive as you forgive. Strengthen my faith Father so that when I pray, I believe in my heart that it is already done. You are the author and finisher of my faith and so I ask that you help me not to waver in it. I need you now Lord, I am ready to move past this pain, and receive all that you have for me. I love you and I can't make it without you. I ask all these things in your son Jesus name Amen.

28 Days of Refining, Renewing, Restoring and the Refreshing

Day 10

Isaiah 43:19 New Living Translation (NLT)

For I am about to do something new. See, I have already begun! Do you not see it?
I will make a pathway through the wilderness. I will create rivers in the dry wasteland.

I prayed more than I had ever prayed in my life and asked God to help me renew my mind, and after a few months, I began to see the change in my thoughts. God was doing a new thing in me and I couldn't describe the feeling. All I knew was I had taken on a new attitude toward life, and in turn, I was getting a part of my life back that I had given away to the pain. God was doing just as the scripture says by making a pathway for me to walk straight through the wilderness of my pain, and all the places that seemed to dry up like my dreams, my joy, my laughter, there He created a river.

The wilderness defined is a place of danger, temptation, and chaos, it is also a place for solitude, to be nourished, and to receive revelation from God. It is an in-between place where life as we know it has been interrupted which can cause a person to be thrown off, stagnant or on hold from the path they originally started on. It can also be a place where you find yourself; strengths and weaknesses, and new possibilities are presented. By God giving me a pathway through this wilderness at a time where my life had been put on hold, and suspended; my identity shifted from a child that God was punishing to a child of His that he loved, and from that point the possibility and thought of me living again was birthed, and my dried up wasteland was flowing with running rivers.

Before his passing, there were things I use to dream about doing with my life.

Life After Death: Growing Past the Pain

I wanted a musical career, and to go back to school to be a paralegal. I wanted to have more children, but by allowing the pain to control me I had given up on my vision. My life had completely changed but my dreams didn't have too.

Don't allow the pain that you are feeling to become a hindrance. Whatever the plans were for your life, they are still possible, and even though they might look different due to not having that person we love to be a part; we still have to believe that together with God, we can! Start to remember again, dream and most importantly live! This is the only life we get so let's live it to the fullest.

Prayer

Lord, I thank you for my wilderness experience. I thank you for creating rivers in the dry places of my life. It is because of You that I can dream again. It is because of You that my thoughts have been renewed and today I just want to say thank you for doing a new thing in my mind and in my life. I love you and I can never make it without you, and I pray all these things in Jesus name. Amen.

28 Days of Refining, Renewing, Restoring and the Refreshing

Day 11

Psalm 139:16 New Living Translation

You saw me before I was born. Every day of my life was recorded in your book. Every moment was laid out before a single day had passed.

About a year ago, I was in the process of starting my own business, and in the planning stages, I was told to plan on losing as well as gaining. I had to plan for the hard times as well as the good because things happen. At first I thought "why am I planning to fail before I even get started," but my mentor told me that It wasn't that I was planning to fail, I just had to be prepared for times that my business wasn't doing so well so that I wouldn't be caught off guard when a loss happened. This was just a part of the process that I would have to endure.

I didn't think about losing him not even once during the 13 months he was with me, neither did I plan on it. I had experienced loved ones dying, but never this close to home. I didn't know to plan for him leaving me especially when I had not had that much time with him. How do we prepare to live without someone we love? How do we prepare for the report from the doctor, or carrying a baby for months only to find that the heart has stop beating while in the womb, and the happiness and anticipation of the arrival of your baby is not the joyful one you planned. This was a question that I pondered on for years, and came to realize that death is a part of the process and even though we will never be ready to let go of the ones we love, we can still prepare our mind according to the word of God, and making sure that we make the most of time that we were allotted to spend with our loved ones so that there is no regret when they leave.

Life After Death: Growing Past the Pain

Just like with the business, we have to plan on losing especially when we know beforehand that loss will occur. Just as there was a time to be born, there is a time to die and this was a part of the plan from the beginning. He gave us time to love on those close to us. Sometimes we do and sometimes we don't because of petty arguments, holding grudges over small things; having family members that we haven't spoken to for years over a misunderstanding, or friends that we have had from childhood but we allowed miscommunication to separate us. When we have these unresolved issues with our loved ones and they pass away we are left feeling guilty or saying that "life is too short." The bottom line is that we are poor managers of our time and didn't spend it wisely. Remember the scripture says that every moment was laid out, so with that being said make sure that we are making the most of these moments so that during the grieving process we are not dealing with guilt as well.

Today, let's plan to spend time with our loved ones knowing that every second counts. We may have been caught off guard this time, but we will be more strategic when it comes to our time. . Having a renewed mind allows us to accept His strategic plan for our lives, and we will better be prepared to embrace what was, and continue on to what will be, right in the midst of our pain.

Once the renewing takes place we repair our thinking as God repairs what has been broken, He mends the broken heart by re-establishing or bringing us back into original existence, use, function, or position. He loves us extremely too much to leave us stuck or paralyzed by the cares of this life. The scripture says that He came that we have life, and life more abundantly and He wants us to live our best life. Holding on to the fact that no matter the circumstance we are facing, He can make us anew again; vibrant and full of life if we would only allow ourselves to be renewed in our thinking, mindset, and our spirits.

28 Days of Refining, Renewing, Restoring and the Refreshing

Today, let's start to change our thinking by not focusing on what went wrong or what we have lost; but shift our focus to all of the things that have gone right in our lives and all the things that we have gained. What have we been blessed with even after we have lost something or someone? I lost my firstborn, but God turned around and blessed me with four more children that were healthy. Three daughters ages 24, 21, and 18; and another son who is now 17 years old. Not one of my children could ever replace Baby Sean, but the opportunity was presented to me and I recommitted to being a mother again. It was definitely hard because I was consumed with worry for them, but instead of turning away from God, I turned to Him for the renewal of my strength, and I prayed daily for the renewing of the mind.

Prayer

Lord, today we say thank you. Thank you for the time that you have given us, every second that you planned out for us. We ask today that you help us to be more strategic with our time so that we don't waste precious moments. Continue to renew us in our minds and hearts, Lord, give us strength for the journey. Lord we trust the plan that you have for our lives you and could never make it without you, and we pray all these things in your precious son Jesus name Amen.

Life After Death: Growing Past the Pain

Day 12

Ecclesiastes 3:12 New Living Translation

So I concluded there is nothing better than to be happy and enjoy ourselves as long as we can.

By being able to change my thinking I was able to talk about him more remembering the times we had. Thinking back to his birth and still remembering that day as one of the happiest days of my life. It still hurt not being able to kiss his sweet little lips or comb his hair while he's singing a song that I wasn't able to make out. How he would run and get his little police car every time my nephews Geo and Sergio would come to visit him, and they would play with him for hours. These memories kept him alive in my heart, and they are memories that I will forever cherish of my baby boy.

I remember when he learned the song " Ooh Eeh Ooh Ah Aah Ting Tang Walla Walla Bing Bang," and his dad and I would sing right along with him as if it were our favorite song. Oh, how I remember that there was not one Barney song I didn't know because that's all he watched. How he had all of the Chicago Bulls gear because his dad and mom were die-hard Bulls fans. It is only with the renewing of the mind that I am able to share these memories and thoughts with others about him without feeling any guilt, knowing that It was planned out from the beginning of time, the day that he would leave us. I rest in knowing that it was not my fault, but God's plan. I had a dream for his life, but God's plan trumps my dreams any day.

Today, let's try to get one memory of time spent with that loved one before their passing, or that spouse before the divorce. That memory of the wedding or honeymoon, when you first found out you were expecting, or a pleasant memory of your life before the diagnosis. Think back to the times you were happy, talk about it, laugh at that joke that they told you. Whatever it is, get it in your mind allowing it to replace the negative thoughts that take you back to a place of pain. If today is still too hard for you, then try again tomorrow. The point is to push past your pain with everything you got so that you too can begin to smile again and enjoy the happiness that life brings for as long as you can.

Prayer

Father, I thank you for Your lovingkindness toward me. I thank you that when before I was even conceived, you had planned out my life for me. You planned the happy times as well as the sad times, knowing that I could handle it and make it through with You as my guide. Although I may still be hurting, I have allowed You to work in my heart and my thoughts, and because I have done so, you have given me understanding and I thank you for it. I will always cherish the memories You gave us and the time I got to spend with my loved ones. I will enjoy life for as long as I can and appreciate every moment You have blessed me with. I thank you for what was and praise for what will be and I celebrate it all in Jesus name. Amen.

Life After Death: Growing Past the Pain

Day 13

Matthew 6:27 New Living Translation

Can all your worries add a single moment to your life?

As I was asking God to renew my mind, part of me was still worried about having other children and the same thing happening. Exactly two years after my son passed away, I gave birth to a baby Girl named Chaneka Monae Hardin January 23rd, 1994. This is actually the day before Baby Sean's birthday, he was born January 24th, 1992. Look at God! I was more stressed during this pregnancy than I had ever been in my entire life. I was worried about losing her more than I was enjoying the thought of having her. Here I was, 2 years past the date of his death and still hindered by the pain. When she was born, I focused more on losing her than loving her and it was literally killing me.

When she would sleep I would be awake. When she was awake I would be awake. I wasn't sleeping at all trying to stay awake so that I could make sure that she was breathing. This was stressing me to the point that I ended up in the hospital. The entire left side of my body went numb and the doctor had to tell me to take a vacation away from my baby because I was killing myself. When I left the hospital, I began to pray and every scripture that I stored up in my heart came to my remembrance. I would repeat these scriptures whenever I would feel myself stressing and eventually I wasn't worried anymore. My trust and faith in God had kicked in.

Worry doesn't change the situation, but it can surely change and alter our faith. Today, if you are still struggling with moving past the pain, revisit the previous scriptures that we went through at the beginning of the book, and pray and ask God for what you need. Remember call Him who you need Him to be, believing that He will show up and do exactly what He said He would do.

28 Days of Refining, Renewing, Restoring and the Refreshing

Prayer

Father, I come to you today asking that you regulate my thoughts, and increase my faith. Your word says that you are the author and finisher of my faith so my very belief in You, comes from You. Lord, I need you to help remove all worry and to stand on your word. I Love you and I can never make it without You, and I give You all the honor glory and praise. In Jesus name, I pray Amen.

Life After Death: Growing Past the Pain

Day 14

Isaiah 1:18
"Come now, and let us reason together

As we are transitioning to the restoring phase I want to leave you with a quote...
"Where there ought to be the greatest force of reasoning, there is the greatest corruption that weakens all things."-Anonymous

This corruption could be worrying, fear, guilt, shame, and anxiety can all weaken our faith and cause us to doubt God and his ability, and also doubt the plan that he established for our lives. Think good thoughts, focus on the good news, don't look at what you have lost, but thank God for all that you have gained. Reason by way of the scriptures and what you know to be true according to His word. Meditate on Proverbs 3:5-6 and pray and ask God to regulate your thoughts, as He renews your mind.

28 Days of Refining, Renewing, Restoring and the Refreshing

Restoring

Restoring which is the third phase of this devotional is where we are being restored back to the state that we were in previously. Where we were before the pain, before the divorce, or the report from the doctor. This process can only take place once we have accepted the fact that this all is not only a part of life, but a part of our process and the only way to be restored is through Christ our Savior. No antique has ever restored itself, because if it were up to the item it would only get worse. Understanding that we can do nothing independent of God, causes us to rely on Him at all times, and in all situations. So, whatever you may be facing believe that He is able to restore all that was lost in the fires of life if only you trust Him. Meditate on these scriptures just as I did and they will serve as reminders of God's unfailing love for you.

Day 15

1 Peter 5:10

In his kindness, God called you to share in his eternal glory by means of Christ Jesus. So after you have suffered a little while, he will restore, support, and strengthen you, and he will place you on a firm foundation.

To restore means to return to an earlier condition. To give back something that was taken or lost. In my case, there were things that I lost and the things I felt had been taken from me due to the death of my son. I felt my joy had been taken along with my son, I wasn't living, I was only existing, I, at one point lost my faith oh but God will restore you as the scripture stated. The suffering only lasted a little while, and before I knew it, the things I lost were being restored.

God had refined me to get the impurities out of me, then my mind had to be renewed so that when He restored what had been taken and lost, I would not only be able to receive it, but I would have the ability and the strength to maintain it. I lost one child and over time gave birth to 4 more, and God is so strategic that two of my children that were born after the passing of my son, were born the day before his birthday. The reason I find this amazing is that I would have been mourning on his birthday, but God gave me something to rejoice over at that moment. I cried on his birthday still, but it was only because I have seen the hand of God in my situation.

Both, my oldest daughter Chaneka, and my youngest, my son Eugene were given to me on January 23rd so, instead of crying and being sad over his loss, I had a reason to rejoice and give thanks. Because it is the Lord that giveth and the Lord that taketh away. He

28 Days of Refining, Renewing, Restoring and the Refreshing

took away my sorrow and restored my joy. I had a reason to go on and live the best life possible. It was not by chance that they were born the day before he was. They both were due in February, but God in his planning saw fit to have it happen in His timing.

I felt strengthened again, I was supported by not just those around me, but God was with me. My faith was fully restored and I wanted to live. God will restore us to a settled and peaceable condition, and perfect his work in us if we only trust Him. He will strengthen us when we are weak and place us on a solid foundation. The older saints use to say "He picked me up, turned me around, and placed my feet on solid ground." Now I can bear witness to this because that is exactly what He has done for me. If he did it for me, know that He is Able to do it for you!

Today, know that God is God and that the suffering will only be for a little while. Trust that this pain is only temporary, and after a while, you will be established and made great because of all you've had to endure. God loves you!

Life After Death: Growing Past the Pain

Prayer

Lord, I thank, and praise you on today for the wonderful things you have done. For being my support, my strength, and for restoring the joy of my salvation. Thank you for being my refuge that I can run unto and find safety. Thank you, Lord! I know that This too shall pass, that this will last only for a little while. Lord continue to increase my faith as I continue to grow closer to you. Thank you for comforting and keeping me, and though I can never repay you for all that you have done, I will continue to lift you up through my serving, my praise, and my worship. I love you and I could never make it without you. I ask all these things in Jesus mighty and majestic name Amen.

28 Days of Refining, Renewing, Restoring and the Refreshing

Day 16

Psalm 71:20 New Living Translation

You have allowed me to suffer much hardship, but you will restore me to life again and lift me up from the depths of the earth.

Not only was God Restoring my joy, but my life was coming back together. The father of my son and I had split up shortly after the birth of my daughter, and I thought "here I am losing something else as well." But just when it seems as if things are falling apart, is when God is putting it all together. I had only had my daughter Chaneka at the time, and I had finally gone back to work at this point and was feeling like I could go on, but then here comes the breakup.

I wasn't looking to be in another relationship, but it was surely looking for me. Now think back to the scripture earlier that said every moment of our lives were laid out and hold on to that. I had a really close friend at the time named Dee, and we were together all the time. Her boyfriend Bernard was the Godfather of my daughter Chaneka. For years I would go over to Dee's house and would ask where Bernard was, and she would respond and say that he was with his friend named Dude. At first, I thought she just didn't want to tell me the guys name, but they actually call him Dude. For about 5 years I would never see this friend of Bernard's named Dude until one day I went over to Dee's and he answered the door. That moment had been planned and I was not to meet him a moment sooner. God is amazing!

Long story short, this Dude ends up being my husband and giving me 3 beautiful children. Chaneka was five months old at the time we met, but that made no difference, he loved my baby as if she was his, and always has. I lose my son, but I am blessed with three beautiful and healthy children Stacia Winters who is now 21 years old, Deja

Life After Death: Growing Past the Pain

Winters 18, and Eugene Winters III who is 17. So, I lose my boyfriend of 6 years, but I am blessed with a husband. A husband that had a family that not only embraced me and my child but made us a part of their family for real. The dude who's real name is Eugene, and his mother Jeannie not only knew God, but their faith in Him, knowledge of Him and relationship with Him was intriguing to me. They taught me things I never knew about God. They were truly a heaven send into my life. God was not only restoring my life, but He was lifting me up to where I needed to be in Him, using my new family.

Today, all I can say is trust in the Lord. He knows what is best, and if He said that He will restore us life again after the suffering, He's going to do just that. I am a witness.

Prayer

Thank you, Lord, for restoration, and for giving me the opportunity to live again in you. Help me to trust in you and your word, and to stand firm on it. I thank you that what seemed to be falling apart is now coming together, and again I just want to say thank you, Lord. In Jesus name, I pray. Amen.

Day 17

2 Corinthians 13:9 English Standard Version

For we are glad when we are weak and you are strong. Your restoration is what we pray for.

In the restoration process, old vintage items are taken and transformed into something shiny to the point that it looks new again. Sometimes without knowing the item has been restored, you would think that it is brand new and would never guess that it had been through the process. Well, that's how it was for me. God took me and restored me to the point that I looked nothing like what I had been through. No one would have known that I had a son that passed away, or that I had a father that was not present which caused me to be angry and saddened. Or the fact that I almost had a stroke worrying about death all the time.

When God restores us after being weakened by the storms of life, He gives us back that peace and joy that can only be found in Him. He restores us physically, emotionally, and spiritually to the point that we look better off than before. The scripture says "Your restoration is what we pray for," And David in the book of Psalm chapter 51 did exactly that. David asked God to "restore to me again the joy of salvation," Always pray for what you need from God believing in your heart that it is already done.

Today, if you don't feel as if you've been restored, pray and ask God to restore you to the point that no one would be able to tell what you've been through. We can't restore ourselves, but we definitely serve a God that can!

Life After Death: Growing Past the Pain

Prayer

Father God I'm coming to you today to say thank you! I thank you for your power and ability to restore me mentally, physically and spiritually. I thank you for your willingness to do so even when I doubted you. When my faith was wavering and I was about to give up. Father, I thank you that in all my wanting to give up you never did. I thank you for your power, you strength and the power of prayer that you have given me that allows me to petition you for what I need, and who I need You to be. I pray that you cover and keep me, and I pray all these things in your son Jesus name Amen.

28 Days of Refining, Renewing, Restoring and the Refreshing

Day 18

Today I want you to write in your favorite scripture that pertains to where you see yourself now in this process. After you have found that scripture write how you can apply it to your life now.

_____
_____
_____
_____
_____
_____
_____
_____
_____
_____
_____
_____
_____
_____
_____
_____
_____
_____
_____
_____

Life After Death: Growing Past the Pain

Day 19

James 1:17 New Living Translation

Whatever is good and perfect is a gift coming down to us from God our Father who created all the lights in the heavens

One of the first questions I had, when he passed away, was "why me?" I repeatedly asked the Lord this question, but as the healing process continued and I began to get closer to the Lord, I gained an understanding. But this was not the only thing I gained. There were certain gifts and talents that I didn't know that was in me, and I had no idea that creativity could be birthed out of pain.

As I came across this very familiar passage of scripture, the question I had changed from "why me" to why not me." The pain that I had experienced gave birth to creativity. I began to write, never even knowing that I had the ability. I wrote songs and poems, and actually shocked myself to learn that I had this gifting. One day while I was thinking about my son, I had the urge to write so, I picked up a pen and grabbed some paper and watched my heart transform into a melody. It was a beautiful song written about my son, and God knew that from the pain I experienced that I would tap into my gifts, and He knows this because He was the giver of this gift. The scripture says that "every good and perfect gift is coming from the Father," and then it goes on to say "who created all the lights in heaven." When I hear this scripture it takes me back to what my pastor Bishop Robert L. Green use to say when he told us" that everything that God created solves a problem.; and when God created light, He solved the problem of darkness." This stood out to me in a sense that the gift that God gave me was to help to solve a problem for the many of us that get stuck in our pain, and loss and do not know how to move forward.

28 Days of Refining, Renewing, Restoring and the Refreshing

God knew the gifting that He had given me to write, would produce this book and would help others.

I thank God for restoring me and allowing my mind to be transformed so that I could see my pain as my process, recognize the gifting that was birthed from that pain, and use my light to help someone else. The God we serve is amazing, and my suffering was not in vain. I hope so far, that hearing about my story, and how God brought me through the different stages inspires you to listen for the gift being sent from heaven, and then let it be the solution for someone else. Pay it forward today.

Today, allow that good and perfect gift from the Lord to be a light to someone else. God will restore us to the point that those that are looking on won't even believe that we have even been in the fire, to begin with. What is the gift that God has given you to serve as a solution to someone else that may be in the fire? I admonish you to search within and listen to the voice of the Lord so that you know too, which way to go.

Prayer

Father, I thank You that you are the giver of our gifting and that you allow us to utilize our gifts for edifying and to assist others through whatever process they might be going through. Lord, please help me to not only use my gift but to be able to identify it. Continue to give me the tools that I need to be that light for someone else in a dark place that they might be in. Lord, I love you and I ask all these things in Your Son Jesus name Amen.

Life After Death: Growing Past the Pain

Day 20

Philippians 4:6 New King James Version

Be anxious for nothing, but in everything by prayer and supplication, with thanksgiving, let your requests be made known to God;

During this process of restoring, understand that prayer has to serve as the maintenance during it. Even though an item has been restored, you still have to work to keep it in good condition. When a computer is refurbished, it still has to be rebooted and the virus protection is needed. When an engine to a vehicle has been rebuilt, an oil change is still in order or the engine will blow. It is the same once we have been refined, renewed, and restored. The scripture says to "not worry about anything, instead pray about everything." So there will be different situations that arise that cause pain for us or cause us to develop fear after we have moved past the previous situation.

My pain didn't just stop with the death of my son or my divorce, but right in the midst of writing this book I was tested and tried again. I received a report from the doctor saying that I had blood clots in my lungs, and there was a visible sign of the blood clot in my leg. At first, when the doctor told me that the test came back positive for the blood clots, I begin to cry and became worried. I had heard of people dying from this, and my friend and sister in Christ Ketrena Jones was on the phone with me when the doctors told me this, and she immediately went into prayer. She believed God and that the test was going to come back negative, but it's something different when you're sitting in the hospital and on the receiving end of the report. When I hung up the phone from her I started to cry out to God asking him to show Himself strong. I had heard my pastor Bishop Robert L. Green's mom Cluster Bailey say that with such authority and I was an eyewitness to His strength being manifested at that very moment. so I said it myself in prayer.

28 Days of Refining, Renewing, Restoring and the Refreshing

I told the Lord that I still had too much work to do, and I called Him who I needed Him to be. "Healer!"

The doctor had them do an ultrasound on the visible blood clot in my leg, and then they did a CT Scan for the lungs. When the results came back, there was no blood clot in my leg. Yeah that's right you could see it but it wasn't there! Then the CT Scan showed no sign of blood clots in my lungs although the test came back positive prior to the scan. There was never a need for me to worry, only a need for me to pray, just as I had done before when I had to pray for strength after the death of my son. He who promised is faithful! Trust Him, because no matter what I have been through He has always been right there.

Today, whatever it is whether divorce, a report from the doctor, finances or the loss of a loved one, pray about it and don't worry at all, you're in Good hands. God's hand and they are unfailing.

Prayer

Father, I come to you today thanking you for the power of prayer. I thank you that You are always willing to meet me where I am and that I have the ability to bring everything to You in prayer. Father, I thank You that even when I don't know what to pray for, the Holy Spirit intercedes on my behalf. I thank You for every answered prayer, and your listening ear and I ask that you continue to dwell with my mind, body and spirit in Jesus name I pray Amen.

Life After Death: Growing Past the Pain

Day 21

Philippians 4:7 New King James Version

And the peace of God, which surpasses all understanding, will guard your hearts and minds through Christ Jesus.

After all that has been said thus far, all that I have endured I still have my joy and I still have my peace. This peace truly surpasses all understanding, because it is amazing to me that after all that I have endured, I have not lost my mind. My father walking out, the death of my son, the death of my marriage and there are also countless other things not mentioned in this devotional that caused me to endure pain like the death of my self-esteem due to being in an abusive relationship, the death of my dreams; I mean you name it I experienced it. But God…

We can't get this type of peace on our own. This peace doesn't come from being optimistic, or when everything is going right. It comes from trusting God and knowing that He is in control. Our destiny has already been planned out so always guard your heart, never allowing anxiety to overtake you. God has you and you are going to be okay because He said it.

Today, pray for peace, and in peace seek understanding of your situation, and you might not always understand why God allows the things that He does, but as long as you trust Him, you know that in the end, it all works out for your good.

28 Days of Refining, Renewing, Restoring and the Refreshing

Prayer

Lord, thank you for loving me, and caring for me and always protecting me from even myself. You never allow me to get so far that I can't hear your voice. In your voice, there is peace, a peace that I can't even explain but I know comes only from You. Continue to regulate my thoughts as I keep my mind stayed on You. I love You, and I thank you in Jesus name I pray Amen.

Life After Death: Growing Past the Pain

The Refreshing

Refreshing defined is "to restore strength and animation; to revive, or to freshen up. After all that you have endured the restoring of your strength is vitally important if you're going to live your best life. There is no better feeling than after you have spent the entire day cleaning, and doing laundry, cooking and taking care of your family, than when you get in that shower freshen up and put on comfortable clothes to lounge around in because it's time to relax. The work has been done and all is taken care of. Well, that's what the refreshing is about. You have been through the fire, changed your thought process, have been restored, now it's time to relax in the refreshing. Looking back and thanking God for helping you complete the work that brought you to this point.

Day 22

Acts 3:16 New Living Translation

The name of Jesus has healed this man, and you know how lame he was before

The more I prayed the more I was restored and the more that I was restored the more peace I had. The people around me didn't know what to think after while because I didn't have the appearance of a mother in mourning anymore. I was sad because I missed my son, but at this point, God had done the work of refreshing me. People would often ask how do I make through the day, and just as in this scripture where Peter had addressed the crowd after they saw the man that had been lame from birth, be healed. Peter told the crowd "why do you look at us as if we made this man walk by our own power and godliness."

There is truly "something about the name Jesus!" There's breakthrough, deliverance, and healing in His name. I constantly called upon the name of Jesus and just as Peter stated, I say to you "it is not by any power or godliness that I am healed, but by the name of Jesus Christ." When I used His name in Faith, not only did He heal me, but He Refreshed my soul! Refreshing is giving one strength or energy, so I not only feel like I can go on, but I have moved on from my pain. It took me some time to get to this point, but I'm here and I owe it all to my Savior Jesus Christ. I can now relax in His love and peace knowing that He is mine and I am His. This thought alone is refreshing to my soul.

Life After Death: Growing Past the Pain

Day 23

Proverbs 11:25 New Living Translation (NLT)

The generous will prosper; those who refresh others will themselves be refreshed.

It is an amazing feeling for me to serve others, and an even better feeling when I can serve someone while I'm going through a storm. At first, I would offer to help others to get my mind off of what I was dealing with until one day someone really needed me to be there but it was painful for me to do so. I had this neighbor who was dealing with the loss of her newborn, and to see her broken and hurt like that took me back to a place where I didn't want to return. Soon after entering her apartment, I don't know what had taken over me but I no longer thought for one minute about my pain, it was more important to me to be there for her.

I would go to her house every day to help try and cheer her up. I would help her clean and talk to her about my experience and how I made it through. Eventually, she didn't seem so depressed and would begin to talk about her daughter. I would clean and help with her kids, you know lighten her load just as others had done for me. What I didn't know is that in serving while in my pain, allowed me to prosper. All type of blessings were coming my way. I didn't need or want for anything; any job I applied for was mine. In helping her to feel refreshed again, I was refreshed as the scripture says, and that is a blessing. I didn't realize that I had been refreshed until I realized that I had been strengthened. Strengthened enough to help someone else through what had me stuck. God is amazing!

28 Days of Refining, Renewing, Restoring and the Refreshing

Today, although you may still be dealing with the pain from your situation, try serving someone else through your pain. Once you refresh and give strength to others the same will come to you. Serving in your pain may sound difficult to do, but trust me I was blessed in the process.

Prayer

Father God, I come asking for your strength today. Strengthen me so that I can be a blessing to someone else during this difficult time. Help me to be able to serve in my pain, because you said in your word that in doing so I will be refreshed as well. I love Lord and I pray all these things in Jesus Mighty and Majestic Name Amen.

Life After Death: Growing Past the Pain

Day 24

Psalm 116:7 New Living Translation (NLT)

Let my soul be at rest again, for the Lord has been good to me.

It is so amazing to me to look back over my situation, the many times I cried out to the Lord and He heard my cry. How do I know that He heard my cry? I'm glad you asked, because every prayer for peace, and joy, and rest was answered. It is simply refreshing to know that I can go to my Father no matter how big the storm may appear, and He can calm the storm just by saying "peace be still." He is just that powerful.

There will never be a time that you can't reach him. He comes to where you are rather you are discouraged, saddened, lonely, tired, afraid etc. He will be near listening carefully to your prayers answering each one according to the plan and will for your life. I prayed for peace I received it. When I couldn't sleep He gave me rest. When I prayed to not be afraid anymore, he increased my faith and blessed me with more children. He is faithful if only you would trust Him. The Lord has truly been good to me.

Today, no matter what you're facing, know that the Lord can and will give you rest. Rest for your mind, and your body. Rest when you're weary, and burdened. Just trust Him. If He did it for me, He can do it for you, and you soon will be saying as the scripture says "The Lord has been good to me!"

28 Days of Refining, Renewing, Restoring and the Refreshing

Prayer

Lord, I thank you that you are a Father that hears and answers prayers. When I am in trouble you will save me, when I am broken you put me back together again. When I am weak You are strong and when call your name things change. So I thank You for loving me, being an ever-present help in my time of need. I love You and I can't make it without you and I give you all the honor, glory and praise. In Jesus name, I pray Amen.

Life After Death: Growing Past the Pain

Day 25

Romans 8:28 King James Version (KJV)

And we know that all things work together for good to them that love God, to them who are the called according to his purpose.

I had a job once that I absolutely loved and I held that job for 6 years. You could have never told me that I would ever leave this job, but one day I was called into the bosses office and told that someone had made a report against me, and as I listened to the report, I knew it was not the truth. I tried to explain this to my boss but she wasn't having it. She felt as if the person had no reason to lie, so she let me go. Oh how hurt I was. I left her office and got in my car and cried all the way home. It felt as if my world had come to an end, and I thought to myself "what am I going to do?" I'm a single mother with no other income. I have rent, car payment, and other bills, and I was stressed. I didn't see my way out of this hole, but God... I eventually found another job, but the blessing was, this new job would allow for me to connect with people that would not only help me to reach goals that I had set for myself, but they would introduce me to other circles of people that would be instrumental in my process today. I eventually realized that I wouldn't be where I am today if I had not been fired. Even though it was painful, in the end, some good still came out of it.

Just as with my son's death I absolutely loved him, saw no end to us, but end up feeling fired as a parent. The good that came from that was the fact that if I had never experienced that loss. I would not have known about my gifting and talents, I would not have written this book and most importantly you would not be on your way to your healing. So see, it all worked out for the good of those of us that love the Lord. We may not be able to see the good in the situation while we are going through, but eventually, you will come to understand.

28 Days of Refining, Renewing, Restoring and the Refreshing

It is refreshing to know that the hardships, and struggles that I thought would take me out, only made me better and stronger. Thank you, God!

Today, trust that the good along with the bad is working out for your good and that you may not see it yet, but your turn around is coming.

Prayer

I thank you Lord that you cause all things to work together for my good, and even though I may not see it right now, I trust that You are working it out for me. I thank you for keeping me through it all and I pray that you continue to guide me through this process to my purpose. I love You in Jesus name I pray Amen.

Life After Death: Growing Past the Pain

Day 26

Job 22:28 New King James Version (NKJV)

You will also declare a thing, And it will be established for you; So light will shine on your ways.

What are you believing God for at this point in your process? Is it healing, peace of mind, maybe your marriage restored, or your dream brought back to life. Whatever it is, write it out and then decree it and declare that it will be done. Utilize the authority and power given to you by Jesus Christ. Speak it as if it is already so. Then write out your prayer to God and if ever you get discouraged, refer back to this page and try it again.

Day 27

1 Thessalonians 5:18

In everything give thanks: for this is the will of God in Christ Jesus concerning you.

At the end of the day, no matter how much pain I experienced, what I may have lost I give thanks to my Lord and Savior Jesus Christ who willed for my life to go just as it did, and so I give him thanks. I know that the will of God will never take me where His grace won't cover me. I know that His grace is sufficient for me and that in my weakness, His power is made perfect (2 Corinthians 12:9). And still, I give Him thanks

I birthed my baby, I nurtured my baby, I loved my baby, I lost my baby, I had to bury my baby, I mourned for my baby, I miss my baby, I cherish the memories of my baby, and last but not least I chose to live after his death because I know that God willed for me to and my baby would have wanted me to. And in all things, I will forever Give Him thanks.

Life After Death: Growing Past the Pain

Prayer

Thanks for allowing me to love him, Lord. Thank you for the opportunity to parent and nurture, to hold and feed. Thank you for allowing me to be there for his last breath even though it was so hard to see. Thank you, Lord, for being right there with me and never leaving my side Lord. Thank you for every parent that will read this book, that has ever lost a child. Thank you for keeping them. Every person that has lost a loved one or whose marriage died, every mother that had a miscarriage or stillborn birth strengthen them, Lord. Cover and keep them, Father. Send the comfort of your Holy Spirit, and Allow them to feel your hand on their very situation. Father do for them as you have for me. Refine, renew, restore and refresh them. Help them to see the pain as part of their process and not a punishment Lord in Jesus Mighty and Majestic name I pray Amen.

28 Days of Refining, Renewing, Restoring and the Refreshing

Day 28

Philippians 4:8 New King James Version

Finally, brethren, whatever things are true, whatever things are noble, whatever things are just, whatever things are pure, whatever things are lovely, whatever things are of good report, if there is any virtue and if there is anything praiseworthy--meditate on these things.

Once you have been refreshed, your thought process should change. You should no longer be pondering on what went wrong, what you lost, but it is necessary that you meditate on the good things. If you are like me and lost a child and had another, cherish the memory of your child that you lost, but don't forget to thank God for blessing you with another. If the marriage didn't work out, thank god for second chances, looking forward to the future.

Close your eyes for me. Now think of that place that you have always seen yourself before the pain began. That happy place, or that place of success. That dream coming to pass, or that husband or wife you always prayed for. Look at those babies you have seen yourself giving birth to or even that ministry you were looking to give birth to. I need you to look past your NOW to your THERE. Picture yourself there and then Decree it as the bible says and it shall be established. Anything of good report or anything that is praiseworthy, focus on that.

Know that I love you and it is an honor and a privilege that I don't take lightly to be able to share with you my pain, my process, and my healing. To God be the glory for all the things He has done! Be blessed and I pray that this book is a blessing to you.

Life After Death: Growing Past the Pain

I didn't have it altogether, but god held it all together

28 Days of Refining, Renewing, Restoring and the Refreshing

Life After Death: Growing Past the Pain

28 Days of Refining, Renewing, Restoring and the Refreshing

Life After Death: Growing Past the Pain

28 Days of Refining, Renewing, Restoring and the Refreshing

Life After Death: Growing Past the Pain

28 Days of Refining, Renewing, Restoring and the Refreshing

Life After Death: Growing Past the Pain

28 Days of Refining, Renewing, Restoring and the Refreshing

Life After Death: Growing Past the Pain

28 Days of Refining, Renewing, Restoring and the Refreshing

Life After Death: Growing Past the Pain

28 Days of Refining, Renewing, Restoring and the Refreshing

Life After Death: Growing Past the Pain

28 Days of Refining, Renewing, Restoring and the Refreshing

Life After Death: Growing Past the Pain

28 Days of Refining, Renewing, Restoring and the Refreshing

Life After Death: Growing Past the Pain

28 Days of Refining, Renewing, Restoring and the Refreshing

Life After Death: Growing Past the Pain

28 Days of Refining, Renewing, Restoring and the Refreshing

Life After Death: Growing Past the Pain

28 Days of Refining, Renewing, Restoring and the Refreshing

Made in the USA
Columbia, SC
09 October 2018